PROFESSOR COOK'S DYNAMITE DINNERS

Enslow Publishers, Inc.
40 Industrial Road
Box 398
Berkeley Heights, NJ 07922
USA

http://www.enslow.com

This edition published by Enslow Publishers Inc.

All rights reserved.

No part of this book may be reproduced by any means without the written permission of the publisher.

Library of Congress Cataloging-in-Publication Data:

Brash, Lorna.
  Professor Cook's Dynamite Dinners/ Lorna Brash.
   pages cm. — (Professor Cook's ...)
  Audience: 9-12
  Audience: Grade 4 to Grade 6
  Summary: "Over a dozen different dinner recipes and each recipe has a short science bit explaining the mysteries of food" —Provided by publisher.
  Includes bibliographical references.
          ISBN 978-0-7660-4301-5
              1. Cooking — Juvenile literature. I. Title II. Series
          TX 773.S3547 2013
          641.5'622—dc23

                                         2012031115

Future edition:
  Paperback ISBN: 978-1-4644-0547-1

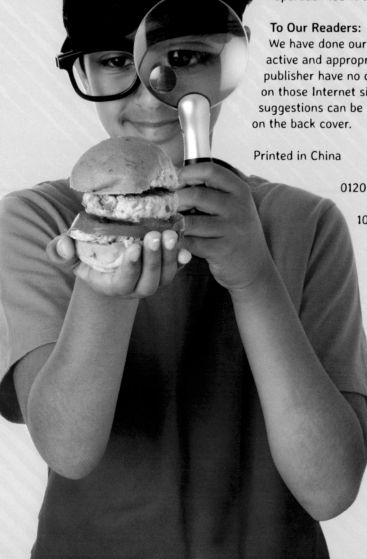

To Our Readers:
We have done our best to make sure all Internet addresses in this book were active and appropriate when we went to press. However, the author and the publisher have no control over and assume no liability for the material available on those Internet sites or on other Web sites they may link to. Any comments or suggestions can be sent by e-mail to comments@enslow.com or to the address on the back cover.

Printed in China

012013 WKT, Shenzhen, Guangdong, China

10 9 8 7 6 5 4 3 2 1

First published in the UK in 2012 by Wayland

Copyright © Wayland 2012

Wayland
 338 Euston Rd
 London NW1 3BH

   Editor: Debbie Foy
   Designer: Lisa Peacock
   Photographer: Ian Garlick
   Proofreader/indexer: Sarah Doughty
   Consultant: Sean Connolly

   Wayland is a division of Hachette Children's
   Books, an Hachette UK company.
   www.hachette.co.uk

CONTENTS

Professor Cook's Incredible Edibles 4

Sticky chicky burger stacks 6

Tex-Mex taco bowl salad 8

Incredible edible bowl soup! 10

Posh fish 'n' chips 'n' dip! 12

Boost your burger! 14

Finger lickin' chicken satay 16

Japan-easy tuna rolls 18

Tongue-tingling sweet and sour noodles 20

Thirsty couscous cakes! 22

Scrambly egg fried rice 24

Superfood cannelloni 26

Chili with a deep, dark secret 28

Professor Cook's Glossary 30

Index & useful web sites 32

PROFESSOR COOK'S... INCREDIBLE EDIBLES

Are you hungry to learn more about your food?

Have you ever wondered why some foods behave the way they do? For example, have you ever wondered how delicious Chinese noodles can taste sweet and sour at the same time? Or have you ever added avocado to your salad and noticed that it turned from green to brown almost immediately?

Well, join Professor Cook and his team to find out the answers to these and many more questions about some of the fascinating ways that our food behaves. Find out what makes a superfood so super, how to make a soup bowl that you can REALLY eat, and find out the deep, dark secret to cooking an amazing chili!

Happy ~~Experimenting~~ Cooking

PROFESSOR COOK'S KITCHEN RULE BOOK

→ Always wash your hands before you start cooking and after handling raw meat

→ Mop up spills as soon as they happen

→ Use oven gloves for handling hot dishes straight from the oven

→ Take care with sharp knives. Don't walk around with them!

→ Switch off the oven or stovetop when you have finished cooking

→ Use separate cutting boards for vegetables and meat

→ Store raw and cooked foods separately in the fridge

→ Don't forget to tidy up the kitchen afterwards! No-brainer, huh?

ABBREVIATIONS

c = cup

tsp = teaspoon

tbsp = tablespoon

oz = ounce

°F = degree Fahrenheit

HOT GOODS!

WHEN YOU SEE THIS WARNING SIGN AN ADULT'S HELP MAY BE NEEDED!

The "Science Bits"

Believe it or not, cooking involves a lot of science! The Science Bits that accompany each of Professor Cook's delicious recipes answer all the mysteries about food that you have ever wondered about. They also explore some of the interesting, unusual, or downright quirky ways that our food can often behave!

STICKY CHICKY BURGER STACKS

Everybody loves a burger! And good, wholesome burgers are made from good quality ground meat. But what is it that gives the burger its shape and what stops it from falling apart on your barbecue grill? Read on...

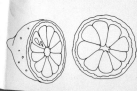

Stuff you need:

16 oz cooked, diced chicken

1 tbsp dark soy sauce

2 tbsp sweet chili dipping sauce

Finely grated rind and juice of 1 lemon

3 spring onions, trimmed and finely chopped

Salt and black pepper

8 little gem lettuce leaves

8 mini soft bread rolls

2 ripe tomatoes, thinly sliced

Makes 8

Step 1

In a large bowl mix together the cooked diced chicken, soy sauce, chili dipping sauce, lemon rind and juice, and spring onions. Season with salt and freshly ground black pepper. Next, get your hands into the mixture and give it a good squeeze until all the ingredients are thoroughly combined.

Step 2

Divide the mixture into 8 equal-sized balls, then flatten them slightly so that you have 8 mini burgers. Place on a baking tray lined with foil.

Step 3

Preheat the grill to hot. Cook the burgers under the grill for 7-8 minutes on each side until cooked through. While the burgers are cooking, split the rolls and tear the lettuce leaves in half. Place one torn lettuce leaf over 8 halves of the rolls. Top with the sliced tomatoes. Place the cooked burgers over the top then add the bread roll tops. Serve with homemade mayonnaise or ketchup (pages 14-15).

The Science Bit

What holds your burger together?

The stuff that stops your burger (as well as people and most animals!) falling apart is a protein called collagen. Ground beef contains collagen, and when it is cooked with a liquid (in this case soy sauce) the collagen is broken down into a softer substance called gelatine (used to make jelly!). This binds the ground beef together and helps your burger to keep its yummy, burger-y shape!

The Science Bit

Why does peeled avocado quickly turn brown?

Avocados (and lots of other fruits) turn brown when exposed to air because of a chemical reaction known as oxidation. But we can help to stop this reaction with a squeeze of lemon juice! Why? Because vitamin C in the lemon juice (called ascorbic acid) slows down the oxidation process and helps the avocado to stay fresh and green for longer!

Stuff you need:

4 large soft flour tortillas
2 tbsp olive oil
1 little gem lettuce
3 1/2 oz cherry tomatoes, halved
1/4 cucumber, finely chopped
14 oz canned mixed bean salad, drained
7 oz sweet corn kernels
1 avocado, cut into chunks and tossed with 2 tbsp lemon juice
4 tbsp vinaigrette dressing
1 3/4 oz Cheddar cheese, grated

Serves 4

Avocados have the highest protein content of any fruit!

TEX-MEX TACO BOWL SALAD

Make your own edible taco bowl to serve this delicious salad! Work quickly with the avocado to keep it looking fresh and green—add it at the end and serve immediately.

Step 1

Preheat the oven to 350°F. Brush the tortillas with oil on both sides and place in heatproof bowls, shaping the sides to make a "taco bowl." Bake for 8–9 minutes until crisp and set into a bowl shape. Allow the taco bowls to cool completely before removing.

Step 2

Shred the lettuce and toss with the tomatoes, cucumber, beans, sweet corn, avocado with lemon juice, and dressing. Spoon the salad into the taco bowls.

Step 3

Finally, scatter the grated cheese over the top and serve!

INCREDIBLE EDIBLE BOWL SOUP!

Here's an amazing fish soup that allows you to eat the bowl AND its contents! And while we're at it, let's have a look at how the haddock gets its lovely smoky flavor...

Step 1

Preheat the oven to 400°F. Pinch a "lid" from the top of the bread roll and set aside. Then scoop out the soft bread from inside leaving a ½-inch layer of bread inside.

When you toast a slice of bread a chemical reaction occurs that alters the sugars and proteins in the bread!

Stuff you need:

6 crusty cob bread rolls
1–2 tbsp olive oil
18 oz potatoes, peeled
1 large onion, peeled
5 c milk
1 garlic clove, crushed
10 1/2 oz canned sweet corn with red pepper, drained
16 oz smoked haddock fillets, skinned
Salt and black pepper
Handful flat-leaf parsley, chopped

Serves 6

Step 2

Brush the insides of the rolls with oil and bake for 15 minutes until golden. This will "seal" the inside of the roll. Chop the potatoes and onion into small chunks and place in a large saucepan.

Step 3

Add the milk to the potatoes and onion and bring to a boil. Turn down the heat, cover, and simmer for 10 minutes.

Step 4

Next, stir in the garlic, sweet corn mixture, and fish. Bring back to a boil, then turn down the heat, cover, and simmer for 5 minutes until the fish flakes easily with a fork. Season to taste with salt and pepper. Stir in the parsley.

Step 5

Spoon the soup into the bread rolls and serve (and eat!) immediately.

The Science Bit

Why do we smoke fish?

Before fridges were invented, freshly caught fish was preserved by smoking it over slow-burning wood chips to stop it from rotting. Smoking absorbs moisture from the fish and inhibits the growth of bacteria, which can cause it to decay. Smoking also stops fat on the surface of the fish "going off" (due to oxidation), and so protects the inside of the fish, which is good to eat!

POSH FISH 'N' CHIPS 'N' DIP!

A fish and chip dinner is a yummy treat – and one that might even help to make you a bit brainier...!

Step 1

Preheat the oven to 400°F. Cut the potatoes lengthways into wedges and toss with the olive oil. Spread into a single layer on a baking sheet, sprinkle with salt and pepper, and roast for 30-35 minutes until crisp and golden.

Stuff you need:

2 large baking potatoes
1 tbsp olive oil
Sea salt and ground black pepper
Small handful watercress
6 tbsp mayonnaise
4 baby gherkins, finely chopped
2/5 c plain flour
2 large eggs, beaten
2/3 c fresh ciabatta breadcrumbs
1/4 tsp cayenne pepper
23 oz skinned haddock, cod, or salmon fillets, cut into strips
4 tbsp sunflower oil, for shallow frying

Serves 4

HOT GOODS!

Step 2

To make the dip, finely chop the watercress and stir into the mayonnaise. Add the gherkins. Chill until ready to use.

Step 3

Place the flour, the eggs, and the breadcrumbs (mixed with the cayenne pepper) into three separate dishes. First, dip the fish into the flour to coat, then into the egg, and finally into the breadcrumbs to coat evenly.

Step 4

Pour about 3/4 in of oil into a deep frying pan and heat until a piece of bread turns golden in 30 seconds. Cook the fish in batches for 2-3 minutes until crisp and golden. Drain on paper towels and keep warm while cooking the remaining fish. Serve hot with the chips and the gherkin mayo dip.

The Science Bit

Does eating fish <u>really</u> make you brainy?

You've heard this loads of times, right? Well, while eating fish won't instantly make your math homework easier, scientists believe there is some truth to it. The "magic" ingredient in fish is omega-3 fatty acids, which are found in all fish but mainly in "oily" fish such as fresh tuna, mackerel, sardines, herring, and salmon!

BOOST YOUR BURGER!

Ketchup-at-home

What's thick and red and great with French fries? Yep, it's tomato ketchup. Make your own super homemade version to serve with Sticky Chicky Burger Stacks (page 6).

Step 1

Place all the ingredients except the sugar into a food processor and whiz to a smooth puree.

Step 2

Pour the puree into a pan and bring to a boil. Sprinkle over the sugar and stir until dissolved. Reduce the heat and simmer for 30 minutes, stirring until thickened. Allow to cool for 5-10 minutes.

Step 3

Pour the ketchup into a clean container. Seal and store in the fridge. Use within 3 weeks once opened.

Stuff you need:

14 oz tomato puree

1 c cider vinegar

2 onions, peeled and finely chopped

1 large potato, peeled and diced

1 3/4 oz fresh root ginger, peeled and finely grated

2 sticks celery, finely chopped

3 garlic cloves, crushed

1 tsp ground cinnamon

1 tsp ground cloves

2 tsp fine table salt

1 tsp freshly ground black pepper

3/4 c dark brown sugar

Makes 2 1/2 c

Homemade Mayo

Q: How do two liquids combine together to make a yummy, thick, and creamy mayonnaise?

A: See "The Science Bit" for an explanation of this kitchen magic!

Stuff you need:

2 egg yolks
1/2 tsp salt
1/2 tsp Dijon mustard
2 tbsp white wine vinegar
1 c vegetable oil
Sauces or herbs

Makes 1 1/2 c

Step 1

Whisk the egg yolks, salt, mustard, and vinegar with an electric whisk until well combined. Add the oil a spoonful at a time and whisk until the mixture starts to thicken. Continue until all of the oil has been used.

Step 2

Flavor your mayo with 1-2 tbsp barbecue sauce, tomato ketchup, or a small handful of chopped herbs, spring onions, or chives.

The Science Bit

How do two liquids combine to make a solid?

Mayo is made from two main ingredients: vinegar and oil. If you shimmy and shake the two together in a jar, then leave them, after a while they will separate back out into oil and vinegar. However, if you add egg yolks, which contain fats, this stabilizes (or emulsifies) the mixture, preventing the oil and vinegar from separating and creating a yummy concoction to spread on your burger!

15

FINGER LICKIN' CHICKEN SATAY

You'll be licking your lips as well as your fingers with these marinated chicken sticks dipped in a perfectly peanutty sauce. It's a promise!

Step 1

Place the bamboo skewers in a shallow dish and spread them into a single layer. Pour cold water over them to cover. Leave for at least 30 minutes to soak.

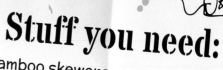

Stuff you need:

12 bamboo skewers
18 oz boneless skinless chicken breasts
4 tbsp soy sauce
1 tbsp runny honey
1 tsp minced ginger
1 tsp minced garlic
Small handful fresh chopped
   coriander
4 tbsp crunchy peanut butter
3 tbsp sweet chili dipping sauce
Lemon wedges, to serve

Makes 12 skewers

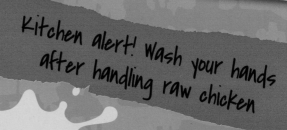

Kitchen alert! Wash your hands after handling raw chicken

Step 2

Cut the chicken into chunks and place in a bowl with 2 tbsp of the soy sauce, honey, minced ginger, garlic, and coriander. Give all the ingredients a good mix. Cover and set aside for 30 minutes.

Step 3

Remove the skewers from the water. Thread the chicken pieces onto the skewers and place on a baking tray. Cook them under a hot grill for 4-5 minutes on each side until golden brown.

Step 4

Place the peanut butter, remaining soy sauce, sweet chili sauce, and 1/3 c water into a saucepan and heat gently until smooth and thick. Serve the satay sticks with the peanut sauce and a squeeze of fresh lemon.

The Science Bit

Can I make healthier peanut butter at home?

Yes you can! Just whiz up 18 oz unsalted shelled peanuts, 2 tbsp peanut oil, and a pinch of salt in a food processor. Keep it in a sealed container in the fridge and use within two weeks. The homemade stuff avoids using sweeteners and preservatives that help to prolong the shelf life of store-bought peanut butter. Overall, your homemade version is much healthier!

JAPAN-EASY TUNA ROLLS

M ade with one of the staple ingredients of Japanese food, sticky white rice, these sushi rolls are easy to eat—even with chopsticks!

Stuff you need:

- 14 oz sushi rice (often called "sticky rice")
- 6 tbsp rice wine vinegar
- 3 nori (dried seaweed) sheets
- 3 oz canned tuna, drained and flaked
- 2 tsp mayonnaise
- 1/2 pimento, deseeded and cut into strips
- 1/4 cucumber, halved lengthways, deseeded and cut into sticks
- Soy sauce, to serve

Serves 4

Step 1

Wash the rice under the cold tap until the water runs clear. Place into a saucepan and add 2 c cold water. Bring the rice to a boil, then cover, reduce the heat, and simmer for 15 minutes. Do NOT lift the lid. Leave the rice to stand for 10 minutes, then stir in the rice vinegar.

Step 2

Place a piece of plastic wrap a little larger than the nori sheet onto a work surface. Place the nori sheet on top. Spoon a third of the cooked rice into the center of the nori sheet and spread to the edges leaving a 3/4-in space along one edge of the nori.

Step 3

Mix the tuna and mayo and spread a third of it across the center of the rice. Arrange a third of the pimento and cucumber sticks along the center of the tuna mixture.

Step 4

Use the plastic wrap to help you roll up the nori. The uncovered strip of nori will make a good "seal" to the end of your sushi roll. Repeat with the remaining ingredients to make two more rolls.

Step 5

Unwrap the rolls and cut each into 5 equal-sized pieces. Dip your sushi pieces into soy sauce, eat, and enjoy!

Wow! Rice husks are so tough that in some countries they are used to make concrete!

The Science Bit

Why is sushi rice so super-sticky?

It's the starch in rice that makes it so sticky. When you cook this short-grain rice, the water and heat soak into the grain and the starch molecules break down and absorb water to form a sticky "gel" (this process is called gelatinization). Sushi rice is cooked using the absorption method, which means no water remains after cooking. So the starch released into the water is then readily gobbled back up by the rice grain making it super-sticky!

TONGUE-TINGLING SWEET AND SOUR NOODLES

Get your taste buds a-jangling with this noodle dish that combines a range of flavors to really tantalize your tongue!

Step 1

Heat the oil in a wok or large frying pan and fry the onion for 3-4 minutes. Stir in the garlic, mushrooms, red pepper, and carrot and stir-fry for 3 minutes more.

Stuff you need:

1 tbsp sunflower oil
1 small onion, chopped
1 garlic clove, crushed
5 oz button mushrooms, sliced
1 red pepper, deseeded and thinly sliced
1 carrot, peeled and cut into sticks
8 oz can pineapple chunks in natural juice
1 tbsp corn starch
Juice of 1 lemon
2 tbsp tomato puree
3 tbsp soy sauce
4 1/2 oz egg noodles
2 spring onions, trimmed and sliced

Serves 4

Step 2

Drain the pineapple chunks, reserving the juice in a measuring cup. Add enough cold water to the pineapple juice to make about 1 c of liquid. Add the pineapple to the stir-fry mixture and cook for 2-3 minutes, stirring occasionally.

Step 3

Meanwhile, mix the corn starch with the lemon juice to form a smooth white paste. Stir in the tomato puree, soy sauce, and pineapple juice liquid.

Step 4

Cook the noodles in a pan of lightly salted boiling water according to the packet instructions.
This should take about 3-4 minutes.

Step 5

Add the noodles to the stir-fry mixture and pour the sauce over it. Turn up the heat and cook for 1-2 minutes, stirring until the sauce has become thick and glossy, coating all the ingredients. Sprinkle with the onions, then eat with chopsticks if you can!

The Science Bit

Can you taste sweet <u>and</u> sour?

Your tongue is covered with tiny little taste sensors called papillae. These detect the molecules in your food that gives it flavor. Scientists believe that we can detect five different flavors with our papillae. These are sweet, sour, salt, bitter, and umami, which is a highly savory, meaty flavor found in such foods as tomatoes and cured meat.

THIRSTY COUSCOUS CAKES!

Couscous is a North African food that is traditionally steamed and served with rich stews. The tiny couscous granules soak up boiling water as if by magic!

Stuff you need:

1 3/4 oz couscous
Large handful fresh coriander, finely chopped
1 small garlic clove, crushed
3 tbsp olive oil
1/2 tsp ground cumin
1/2 tsp ground coriander
2 tbsp pine nuts, toasted
1 3/4 oz feta cheese, finely diced
2 medium eggs, beaten
1 c fine white breadcrumbs
Salt and black pepper
2 tbsp plain flour
4 tbsp sunflower oil, for shallow frying

Serves 4

HOT GOODS!

Step 1

Place the couscous in a large bowl and cover with 1/2 c of boiling water. Leave to stand for 10 minutes, then fluff up with a fork.

Step 2

Place the fresh coriander, garlic, oil, cumin, and ground coriander into a food processor and whiz to a thick puree. Stir into the couscous with the pine nuts, feta cheese, half the beaten egg, and half the breadcrumbs until well combined. Season with salt and pepper. Roll into 8 small balls and then flatten into burger shapes.

Step 3

Put the flour, the remaining egg, and the remaining breadcrumbs into separate dishes (as shown). Dip the couscous cakes into the flour to cover, then into the beaten egg, and finally the breadcrumbs to coat.

Step 4

Heat the oil in a frying pan. Carefully cook the couscous cakes in batches for 3 minutes on each side until golden. Serve with salad and homemade mayonnaise (see page 15).

The Science Bit

Why does couscous grow?

Couscous is granules of semolina made from durum wheat (the same stuff that pasta is made from). Durum wheat is high in gluten, a type of protein. The Latin word gluten means "glue," and that gives us a clue as to why couscous grows, as it attracts and absorbs liquids. When you pour boiling water over the couscous, each granule can absorb its own volume in water, which makes it double in size!

SUPERFOOD CANNELLONI

Bright green spinach is a superhero's staple food as it's jam-packed to the brim with vitamins A and C, plus iron, zinc, and potassium. Go get some on your plate!

Stuff you need:

28 oz baby spinach leaves
Freshly grated nutmeg
6 sheets fresh lasagna
16 oz low-fat cream cheese
2 tbsp olive oil
1 large onion, peeled and finely chopped
2 garlic cloves, crushed
1 red pepper, deseeded and chopped
14 oz canned chopped tomatoes
1 tbsp tomato puree
2 tsp dried Italian herbs
14 oz canned tomatoes
1/2 c vegetable stock
Salt and black pepper
1 3/4 oz grated mozzarella cheese
Basil leaves

Serves 4-6

Step 1

Rinse the spinach well and place in a large saucepan. Heat gently, stirring, until the spinach starts to wilt. Strain out any excess liquid, then add a pinch of nutmeg.

Step 2

Lay the lasagna sheets out on a work surface and spread with the cream cheese to cover. Lay the wilted spinach over the cream cheese.

Step 3

Put the flour, the remaining egg, and the remaining breadcrumbs into separate dishes (as shown). Dip the couscous cakes into the flour to cover, then into the beaten egg, and finally the breadcrumbs to coat.

Step 4

Heat the oil in a frying pan. Carefully cook the couscous cakes in batches for 3 minutes on each side until golden. Serve with salad and homemade mayonnaise (see page 15).

The Science Bit

Why does couscous grow?

Couscous is granules of semolina made from durum wheat (the same stuff that pasta is made from). Durum wheat is high in gluten, a type of protein. The Latin word gluten means "glue," and that gives us a clue as to why couscous grows, as it attracts and absorbs liquids. When you pour boiling water over the couscous, each granule can absorb its own volume in water, which makes it double in size!

SCRAMBLY EGG FRIED RICE

This is a totally dynamite dinner recipe that you can make so quickly and easily! Apart from the juicy chicken and vegetables, the little egg-coated grains of rice are what makes it oh-so special. So, come on, eggs—tell us how you do it!

Stuff you need:

12 oz long-grain rice
2 tbsp peanut oil
2 garlic cloves, crushed
16 oz skinless chicken breasts, chopped
1 red pepper, deseeded and chopped
1 tbsp curry powder
1 bunch spring onions, thinly sliced
2 1/2 oz frozen peas, defrosted
2 tbsp light soy sauce
2 eggs, lightly whisked
Small handful fresh coriander, chopped

Serves 4

HOT GOODS!

The Science Bit
Why do eggs scramble?

Egg is a protein that changes instantly when heat is added. Proteins are made up of long chains of amino acids. When you whisk the white and yolk of an egg together you are creating new chemical bonds between the proteins in the egg white and the proteins in the yolk. Water from the yolk is trapped along with air, which was added when you whisked the eggs. Once heat is added the proteins clump together. If unstirred they form an omelette, but if stirred they form scrambled eggs as you are breaking down the protein connections.

Step 1

Bring a large pan of lightly salted water to a boil. Add the rice and stir with a wooden spoon. Cook for 12-15 minutes. Carefully lift the saucepan and pour the rice into a sieve.

Step 2

Pour the oil into a deep frying pan or wok. Heat gently then add the garlic, chicken, and pepper and stir-fry for 8-10 minutes. Add the curry powder and cook for 1 minute.

Step 3

Add the cooked rice, spring onions, and peas and cook for 5 minutes, stirring occasionally to make sure the ingredients do not stick. Drizzle over the soy sauce.

Step 4

Push the rice mixture to one side of the pan. Pour the eggs into the uncovered part and stir until they scramble, then mix with the rice. Sprinkle with coriander and serve!

SUPERFOOD CANNELLONI

Bright green spinach is a superhero's staple food as it's jam-packed to the brim with vitamins A and C, plus iron, zinc, and potassium. Go get some on your plate!

Stuff you need:

28 oz baby spinach leaves
Freshly grated nutmeg
6 sheets fresh lasagna
16 oz low-fat cream cheese
2 tbsp olive oil
1 large onion, peeled and finely chopped
2 garlic cloves, crushed
1 red pepper, deseeded and chopped
14 oz canned chopped tomatoes
1 tbsp tomato puree
2 tsp dried Italian herbs
14 oz canned tomatoes
1/2 c vegetable stock
Salt and black pepper
1 3/4 oz grated mozzarella cheese
Basil leaves

Serves 4-6

Step 1

Rinse the spinach well and place in a large saucepan. Heat gently, stirring, until the spinach starts to wilt. Strain out any excess liquid, then add a pinch of nutmeg.

Step 2

Lay the lasagna sheets out on a work surface and spread with the cream cheese to cover. Lay the wilted spinach over the cream cheese.

Step 3

Roll up the lasagna sheets from the short end and place in a large ovenproof dish (large enough so that the lasagna rolls are in a single layer).

Step 4

Preheat the oven to 350°F. Heat the oil in a large saucepan and fry the onion, garlic, and red pepper until softened. Stir in the tomatoes, tomato puree, herbs, canned tomatoes, and stock. Bring to a boil, cover and simmer for 20 minutes.

Step 5

Season with salt and pepper and then pour over the cannelloni rolls. Sprinkle over the cheese and bake for 30 minutes until bubbling. Garnish with basil leaves and serve with lots of green salad.

The Science Bit

Why is spinach so good for you?

Spinach is known as a superfood. It is low in calories and packed full of vitamins and minerals. To improve our body's absorption of iron from the spinach, it should be eaten with a source of vitamin C. So, squeeze fresh lemon juice onto cooked spinach before you eat it, or eat your superfood cannelloni with a large glass of fresh orange juice!

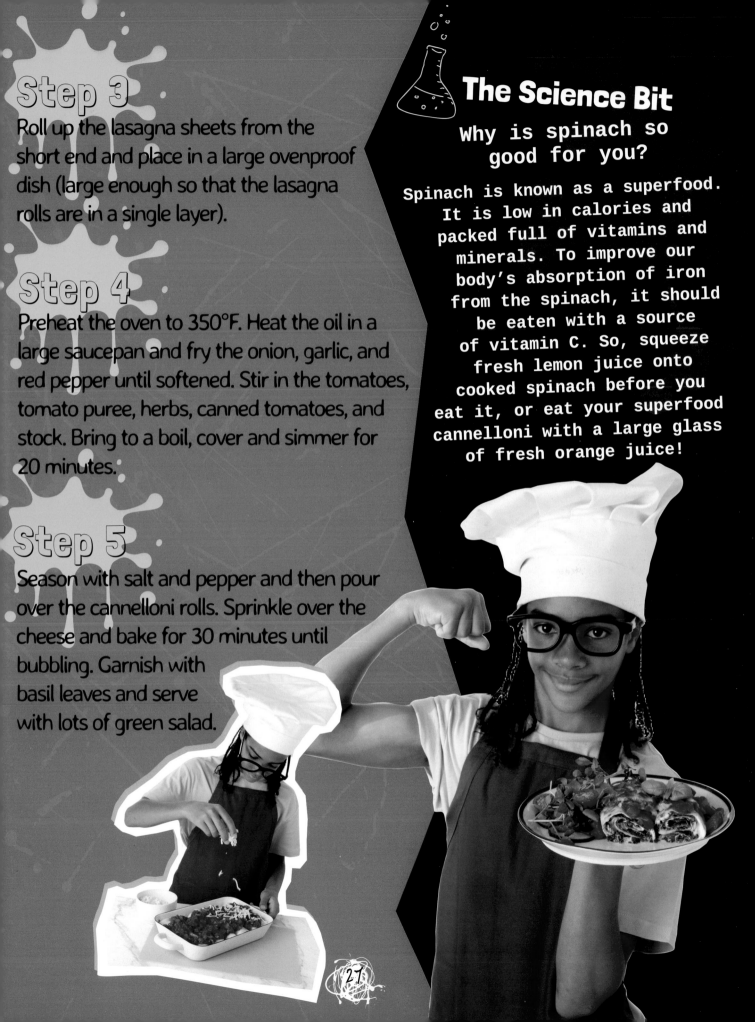

Stuff you need:

2 tbsp sunflower oil
18 oz lean ground beef
2 large onions, peeled and chopped
2 garlic cloves, crushed
1 tsp each ground cumin, coriander, and oregano
1 tbsp mild chili powder
1 red pepper, deseeded and chopped
4 1/2 oz chestnut mushrooms, sliced
2 x 14 oz cans kidney beans, drained
2 x 14 oz cans chopped tomatoes
2 tbsp tomato puree
2 tsp Worcestershire sauce
1 oz dark plain chocolate, finely chopped
Salt and black pepper

Serves 6

The Science Bit

Chilies and chocolate?

You may think the idea of putting chocolate and chilies together a bit weird, but the Mexicans have long since added chocolate to their "mole" (sauces). As a fresh red chili dries it develops a sweet, fruity flavor which, when combined with chocolate, makes an awesome combination. It is also thought that the richness of the melted chocolate helps to tone down some of the heat from the chili.

CHILI WITH A DEEP, DARK SECRET

A big hurrah for chili—served with baked potato, fluffy rice, or any which way. But do you know the secret ingredient that Mexicans add to make the sauce truly rich and creamy?

Step 1

Heat the oil in a large pan and fry the ground beef for 5-6 minutes, stirring occasionally until browned all over.

Step 2

Add the onions and garlic and stir well. Cook for 3-4 minutes stirring now and then. Add the cumin, coriander, oregano, and chili powder and cook for 1-2 minutes. Don't allow the mixture to stick to the bottom of the pan.

Step 3

Add the remaining ingredients and bring to a boil. Season with salt and pepper. Cover and simmer gently for 45 minutes, stirring occasionally. Serve with rice or baked potato.

PROFESSOR COOK'S GLOSSARY

AMINO ACIDS these molecules are the building blocks of protein

BACTERIA tiny living organisms that can grow on food

BAMBOO SKEWERS wooden sticks on which you can thread meat, fish, or vegetables for grilling or barbecuing

CALORIES units of energy that are contained within the food you eat

COLLAGEN a protein found in animal tissue. When heated, collagen turns to gelatine

CORN STARCH a white powder that is used to thicken liquids such as soups, stews, and gravies

EDIBLE something (usually a food substance) that we can eat

ELECTRIC HAND WHISK a handheld mixer with two or three whisks attached

EMULSIFY to add a substance that stabilizes a mixture, for example adding an egg yolk to oil and vinegar, and stops them from separating out. This process is known as emulsification

FRY to cook with oil in a shallow frying pan

GELATINE a setting agent used in many puddings and desserts

MINERALS substances in food that help your body grow, develop, and stay healthy

NORI dried sheets of seaweed used in making sushi rolls

OMEGA-3 FATTY ACIDS found mainly in oily fish, these are essential for growth, brain function, and the nervous system

OXIDATION the reaction that occurs when a food substance is exposed to air

PIMENTO a large red pepper that is generally chargrilled, skinned, and bottled or canned in brine (salt water)

POTASSIUM a mineral found in foods such as avocados, dried apricots, white beans, fish, and dates and which is essential in maintaining the nervous system

PRESERVATIVES substances added to food to prevent it from spoiling

SEASON to flavor food with salt and pepper

SOLID something that is firm and keeps its shape, compared to a liquid, which has to be contained

STRAINING to drain ingredients through a sieve to remove the water

SUPERFOODS nutrient-rich foods that fight off aging and illness. Packed full of vitamins, minerals, and antioxidants, these help the cells in our bodies grow, reproduce, and repair

TOSS to lightly throw ingredients (usually salads) together to properly combine them

WHISK to beat with a light, rapid motion

WOK a large, deep frying pan used in Chinese cooking

INDEX

amino acids 24
avocados 4, 8, 9

bacteria 11
bread 6, 7, 10, 11
burgers 6, 7

calories 27
cannelloni 26, 27
chilies 28
chocolate 28
collagen 7
couscous 22, 23
cutting boards 5

eggs 15, 24, 25
emulsifier 15

fish and chips 12, 13
flavors 21
fridges 5, 11

gelatine 7

hygiene 5

iron 26, 27

ketchup 14, 15
kitchen rules 5
knives 5

mayonnaise 12, 13, 15, 23
meat, raw 5, 16
minerals 27

noodles 4, 20, 21

omega-3 fatty acids 13
oven gloves 5
oven safety 5
oxidation 8

peanut butter 16,17
potassium 26
preservatives 17
protein 8, 10, 24

rice 18, 19, 24, 25

smoking foods 10, 11
solids 15
soup 10, 11
spills 5
spinach 26, 27
starch 19
superfoods 4, 27
sushi rolls 18, 19
sweet and sour 4, 20, 21
sweeteners 17

taste sensors 21
toasting 10

vitamins 8, 26, 27

wheat 23
wok 20, 25

zinc 26

USEFUL WEBSITES

www.spatulatta.com
Get some basic cooking skills under your belt, with step-by-step video recipes and a recipe box that includes options for cooking a meal by choosing a basic ingredient, a type of food, occasion, or particular diet.

www.yummyscience.co.uk
Super-fun science projects to try out in the kitchen using everyday foods. Grow your own crystals with salt, test out the toasting properties of bread, or make your own honeycomb toffee. Some of these recipes call for an adult's help, so always make sure you let an adult know before you start.

www.exploratorium.edu/cooking
Find out how a pinch of curiosity can improve your cooking! Explore recipes, activities, and webcasts that will improve your understanding of the science behind food and cooking.

Discover some more incredible edibles with Professor Cook and the team!

Professor Cook's Dynamite Dinners

978-0-7660-4301-5

Professor Cook's Incredible Edibles!
Sticky Chicky Burger Stacks
Tex-Mex
Taco Bowl Salad
Incredible Edible Bowl Soup!
Posh Fish 'n' Chips 'n' Dip!
Boost Your Burger!
Finger Lickin' Chicken Satay
Japan-Easy Tuna Rolls
Tongue-Tingling Sweet and Sour Noodles
Thirsty Couscous Cakes!
Scrambly Egg Fried Rice
Superfood Cannelloni
Chili with a Deep, Dark Secret
Professor Cook's Glossary
Index & Useful Web Sites

Professor Cook's Mind-Blowing Baking

978-0-7660-4303-9

Professor Cook's Incredible Edibles!
Crimson velvet whoopie pies!
Choccy choux puffs
Exploding cupcakes!
Squidgy widgy custard tarts
Oozing crust pizza
Very berry choco ripple meringues
Kitchen sink potpies
Hot ice cream sparkle
Super seedy flowerpot bread
Stack 'em high cheesy puff pie
Black & blue buns
Stained glass cookies
Professor Cook's Glossary
Index & Useful Web Sites

Professor Cook's Fruity Desserts

978-0-7660-4302-2

Professor Cook's Incredible Edibles!
Tropical fruit with goo-ey chocolate dip
Incredible edible tie-dye ice pops
Icy watermelon fruit slices
Hot pineapple "lollies"
Super blueberry cheesecake
Wobbly strawberry mousse
"Magic" apple & blackberry pudding
Ice bowl fruit salad
Nicey slicey summer fruit jelly
Homemade yogurt with fruit squish
Instant frozen yogurt
Sticky licky banoffee cones
Professor Cook's Glossary
Index & Useful Web Sites

Professor Cook's Smashing Snacks

978-0-7660-4304-6

Professor Cook's Incredible Edibles!
Pop-tastic popcorn
Smashing caramel shards
Ice cream in a bag
Cheese-and-ham-o-rama!
Homemade beans on toast
Oat-so yummy power cookies
"No-cry" onion bhajis & dip
Double-dipped mallow cookies
Mini superhero pies!
Gold bullion honeycomb bars!
Pink fizzbomb lemonade
Big dipper breadsticks
Professor Cook's Glossary
Index & Useful Web Sites